MW01008191

Art Quilts of the Midwest

A Bur Oak Book

Holly Carver, series editor

ART QUILTS
OF THE MIDWEST

Linzee Kull McCray

Foreword by Astrid Hilger Bennett

University of Iowa Press, Iowa City

University of Iowa Press, Iowa City 52242
Copyright © 2015 by the University of Iowa Press
www.uiowapress.org
Printed in the United States of America

Design by Kristina Kachele Design, llc
All photos taken by the artists unless otherwise noted.

No part of this book may be reproduced or used in any form or by any means without permission in writing from the publisher. All reasonable steps have been taken to contact copyright holders of material used in this book. The publisher would be pleased to make suitable arrangements with any whom it has not been possible to reach.

The University of Iowa Press is a member of Green Press Initiative
and is committed to preserving natural resources.

Printed on acid-free paper

Library of Congress Cataloging-in-Publication Data
McCray, Linzee Kull.
Art quilts of the Midwest / by Linzee Kull McCray ; foreword by Astrid Hilger Bennett.
pages   cm. — (A bur oak book)
ISBN 978-1-60938-323-7 (pbk), ISBN 978-1-60938-331-2 (ebk)
1. Art quilts—Middle West—Themes, motives.   I. Title.
NK9112.M295   2015
746.460977—dc23   2014034884

To Paul, for all.

CONTENTS

THE ART QUILT

QUILTING HAS ENJOYED an explosion of popularity in the last four decades. In 1971, in his seminal exhibition Abstract Design in American Quilts, at the Whitney Museum of American Art in New York City, curator Jonathan Holstein displayed large, colorful, traditional quilts on the white walls of one of the world's best-known contemporary art museums. The exhibition inspired many new admirers and adherents. As a young printmaking student at Indiana University, I was no exception. Holstein's small, spare book, *American Pieced Quilts,* led me to abandon traditional elements of composition in favor of the grid of piecework in my new textile work. Quilts and textile work thus became personal for me as well.

In the next decade, quilters would proliferate. Most of them created traditional "pieced" quilts, embracing pattern, symmetry, and repetition. However, smaller groups of these quilters saw the potential for pushing the medium beyond patchwork. Out of this, the art quilt movement was born.

In 1989, the national quilt artist Yvonne Porcella founded the Studio Art Quilt Associates (SAQA), "believing in the need to establish a place for art quilts in the world of contemporary fine art." Her goal was to bring professional standards into the art quilt studio and, in turn, bring that studio into the larger art world by establishing art quilt exhibitions and encouraging permanent museum collections for art quilts.

But what is an art quilt? Let's explore definitions and provenance.

Both traditional quilts and art quilts share fundamentals in their description as layers held together in some way by stitching, knotting, or other means. But that is also where their similarities end.

Historically, traditional quilts were intended to serve a function and could fit Merriam-Webster's description as "a bed coverlet of two layers of cloth filled with padding (as down or batting) held in place by ties or stitched designs." We learn that the word dates to the Middle English *quilte,* meaning "mattress" or "quilt," from Anglo-French *coilte* and Latin *culcita* "mattress." Use of the word dates back to the fourteenth century. Similarly, the concept of piecing a quilt top, or assembling small sections of fabric into one whole cloth, has also been around for centuries.

Traditional pieced quilts were especially popular in the United States, where in pioneer days access to new cloth was limited. In traditional quilting, patterns could be followed faithfully or improvised upon, and color might be dependent on available fabric or chosen specifically for a project. Crazy quilts and commemorative quilts were notable exceptions. Quilts were often executed communally, with a quilt top assembled by one person, and the stitching accomplished as a social experience in a community setting. Quilting was mostly a women's activity involving multiple generations.

In today's traditional quilting, these practices continue to evolve. There is much greater freedom in design, scale, and purpose. Quilts are made by both women and men. The "modern" quilt recently burst upon the scene. According to the Modern Quilt Guild, this kind of quilt embraces functionality, but also asymmetry, simplicity, minimalism, modern art, bold color, and more.

The art quilt, on the other hand, is not made with functional intent. Rather, it is a vehicle for creative expression, usually made by one artist. The art quilt embraces many styles, often as contemporary treatments of older methods such as asymmetry, whole cloth, and embellishment. Artists transform cloth through dyes, painting, printing, and stitching. Art quilt imagery can include narrative storytelling, with photorealistic images of landscapes, people, and domestic and urban scenes, or an exploration of abstraction. Art quilts have even moved off the wall into three-dimensional sculpture, and now embrace nontraditional, nonfabric materials.

Many art quilts are smaller than bed-covering size, and in some contemporary applications the "layers" are not cloth at all, thereby reflecting a current trend toward mixed media in all art forms. The long-time SAQA interpretation referred to a "stitched, layered structure." The more recent SAQA definition opens this up: "The art quilt is a creative visual work that is layered and stitched or that references this form of stitched, layered structure." In short, anything goes, as long as the piece involves conjoined layers.

Being a seasoned art quilter takes a certain skill set shared with any creative artist: independent vision, intuition, determination, discipline, and risk-taking. This is not an easy process. A traditional pattern often yields the anticipated and comforting result. Not so with art quilts. Boundaries must be explored and crossed. Just because an art quilter has taken the nontraditional approach does not guarantee the result will be good art. As in the larger art world, there are many weak examples of art quilts. But there are stellar successes, as judged by audience, curatorial, and critical review.

The American Midwest has always had strong textile communities. Although the creation of quilts may have declined in some parts of the country prior to the 1970s, not so in the Midwest, where making things remained an unbroken tradition. Midwestern quilters and other artists often have a strong relationship to landscape and social groups. Several of the most venerable institutions in the world of quilting are located in the Midwest: the International Quilt Study Center in Lincoln, Nebraska, and Quilt National, a premier juried art quilt exhibition held in Athens, Ohio, to name two. According to the former's website, "The center houses the largest publicly held quilt collection in the world. The more than 3,500 quilts date from the early 1700s to the present and represent more than 25 countries" and include art quilts. Other key textile organizations, such as the Surface Design Association, had their start in the Midwest.

Now it's time to stop talking. It is my pleasure to invite you to take the next step and see for yourself. Explore the rich world of Midwest art quilting as reflected in the pages to come.

ASTRID HILGER BENNETT

INTRODUCTION AND ACKNOWLEDGMENTS

Everything about the Midwest seemed exotic when I arrived more than thirty years ago: spring's lush, ruffled peonies, the incandescence of autumn leaves, even winter's monochromatic scheme. Ten years later, just as it began to feel familiar, I moved back to my home state of California. I was stunned to find that gathering the seedpods of eucalyptus trees or brushing against rosemary plants the size of hedges brought my childhood tumbling back. Bougainvillaea-encrusted houses whose big, single-paned windows eyed the ocean felt comfortingly familiar, while they jarred my Iowa-born husband's sense of residential norms.

These moments came unbidden and led me to contemplate what shapes one's visual preferences. While we're influenced by much more than our physical surroundings, they can't help but get under our skin. *Terroir,* the French word for "sense of place," acknowledges that the melding of soil, sun, rainfall, and mineral content creates in a wine a flavor that distinguishes it from wines whose grapes were grown elsewhere. In similar ways, a region—its geography, weather, people, and culture—may bubble up distinctively in the work of a visual artist or writer. Think of the paintings of Georgia O'Keeffe and Grant Wood or the novels of Willa Cather and Daniel Woodrell.

Characterizing a region is challenging, however, and stereotypes abound. The physical Midwest (defined in this book as Illinois, Indiana, Iowa, Kansas, Michigan, Minnesota, Missouri, Nebraska, North Dakota, Ohio, South Dakota, and Wisconsin) is described in turn as flat, rural, wooded, dry, fecund, rainy, dusty, lush, sere, sweltering, blustery, and icy. There's truth to all those descriptors, and to their effect on the region's population, its values, and its customs. Midwesterners are regarded as friendly, hard-working, boring, uncomplaining, private, and modest. Many of those values and traits have their roots in days gone by, when maintaining goodwill with one's neighbors was a key to survival in good times and bad—joining forces to bring in a harvest or raise a barn, for example, or sharing food and warmth during a blizzard.

Another midwestern trait that grew from necessity is thriftiness, saving things just in case. Quilting was a way to use bits of fabric—scraps of old clothing, feed sacks, worn bedding—to create much-needed warmth. The women who pieced these practical blankets were sometimes able to exert their creativity, manipulating scraps to tweak a traditional pattern or saving enough pieces of a certain color to create cohesiveness.

In addition to these stereotypical traits and a textile tradition, there are many other elements that provide inspiration in the Midwest today. Contemporary midwesterners are more likely to live in a city than on a farm, for example, so urban life is increasingly influential. Artists from various parts of the country, as well as from around the world, make the Midwest their home and bring with them the influences and viewpoints of their particular cultures. Travel and the Internet provide exposure to inspiration of all kinds, including the work of other artists.

As a writer covering textiles, art, and craft, I interview artists and designers from across the United States and around the world. More often than not, I hear comments about their environment's impact on technique and design. New Yorkers cite the 24/7 stimulation of city streets; ocean colors sneak into the palettes of Californians; and Australians say their lack of a quilting tradition gives them freedom to experiment. These place-based perspectives on creativity, along with my experience of moving between California and Iowa, where I once again live, spurred my interest in learning about an environment's influence on art in general, and on focusing the lens of regionalism on midwestern art quilters in particular.

The artists who responded to this book's call for entries—and there were close to a hundred who did—were free to define the aspects of midwesternness that affect their work. During the blind jurying process in which the visual artists Emily Martin and Mary Merkel-Hess and I narrowed the submissions to the twenty included artists, we learned that the Midwest's quilt artists react to a wide range of subjects, from the injustices of the current or historical world to something seen on vacation. Some find the visual and emotional landscape of daily life—weather, gardens, neighbors (or lack of them), community events, food—a prime motivator. Additional midwestern influences that were cited include corporations, coal mines, feeling at odds with surrounding stoicism, pedestrian commutes, and contaminated water.

In addition to wondering how these regional attributes and events affected their work, I was curious to learn why these artists chose to express themselves with textiles. Some started (and continue) as painters, sculptors, jewelers, printmakers, and photographers, while others began as conventional quilters; few felt satisfied working within the bounds of tradition. Classes, museum exhibitions, and conversations provided the spark for a shift to art quilting, as did hours spent alone with a needle and thread. Fabric was hailed for its tactile qualities, texture, malleability, worker-friendliness, ease of storing and transporting, and relatively inexpensive cost and availability.

Textiles also are closely aligned with women's work, and these art quilters expressed a variety of viewpoints about this. Some choose it for that very reason, highlighting the connection and honoring the women who came before. Others chafe at the association, wanting to be clear that their art is not to be confused with craft. For still others, it doesn't matter—the medium does what they want it to: readily accepts dye, is easy to manipulate in a studio or home setting, is portable, and best enables them to express themselves.

In order to write the biographies that accompany the artists' work, I shared an hour-long conversation with each of them. I am endlessly fascinated by what drives artists to create, and these talks never failed to provide me with a new perspective. The intent of these biographies is not to duplicate the artists' resumés. Their work appears in juried shows and publications, in public and private collections. They teach students of all ages and abilities, have written books and articles, and have degrees from prestigious colleges and universities. These facts are available on the artists' websites and blogs, and I encourage you to search them out—you will also learn more about their materials and techniques and see additional examples of their work.

Rather than repeat bibliographical information, my goal was to learn how these artists do what they do and the ways the Midwest affects that. I learned that while some create art that expresses strong childhood memories of earth and sky or honors midwestern ancestors, others find the region influential largely for its lower cost of living, which enables them to more readily pursue their art, or for the summer sun and heat that intensifies their dyes and lets them work outside, avoiding messes and toxicity.

With each interview, my appreciation for the Midwest has grown. Hearing artists talk about light, water, their families and neighbors, the seasons, and the places they walk each morning has increased my regard for my own surroundings. Though I yearn for California's moderate temperature and color during January, these artists remind me that the Midwest has shown me things

I'd never before appreciated: the shapes and forms of leafless trees; fireflies dangling above newly cut grass on a summer's evening; the neighbor who runs his snow blower past my house, clearing my sidewalk; the giddiness of seeing the first snowdrops of spring after a long, hard winter. The artists in this book embrace the climate, the land, the people, and the culture, and if they don't embrace it then they use their art to react to it. Talking with them has been a privilege, and I've learned a great deal. I hope you will, too.

For helping me bring this book to fruition, I'd like to thank Emily Martin and Mary Merkel-Hess for their keen eyes and clear, wise communications during the artist selection process and beyond; quilt artist and author Astrid Bennett for her thoughtful essay; Holly Carver and Karen Copp of the University of Iowa Press for their encouragement, for sharing their publishing expertise, and for being a pleasure to work with; Matthew Arant of the University of Iowa Graduate College for technological expertise; my daughters, Maggie and Rebecca McCray, for cheering me along the way, and my parents, William and Sarah Kull, who encouraged my writing when I was young. In particular, I'd like to thank the women who provided the foundation for my love of textiles: my aunt, Marcia Dimmel, who taught me to knit, and my mother, who taught me to sew and who filled our home with beautiful fabrics. Special thanks go to my husband, Paul, for his sense of humor, willingness to read copy, and the occasional, much-needed reality check.

Finally, I would like to thank not only the artists included in the book for trusting me with their insights, but all the artists who took a risk and submitted work for consideration. There were dozens of powerful, artful, and simply beautiful pieces submitted, and I am deeply grateful for everyone's participation.

LINZEE KULL MCCRAY

Art Quilts of the Midwest

Morrison County Wheat Field, 2010
Cotton, machine-quilted
25 by 36 inches

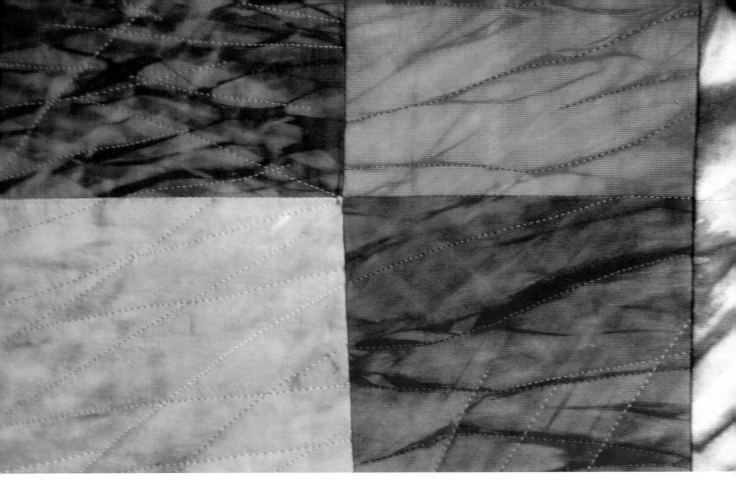

Morrison County Wheat Field, detail

MARILYN AMPE

St. Paul, Minnesota

For Marilyn Ampe, music and art are means to a similar end. "There are chords in music that create an emotional response of bliss, and that's the feeling I'm trying to recreate in my work," says Ampe, an organist at the Church of the Holy Spirit in St. Paul.

Ampe, who grew up on a Minnesota farm, is a painter and former printmaker. But the technique of *arashi shibori,* in which fabric is wrapped around a pole, tied, scrunched, and dyed, enables her to best portray these perceptions. "Fiber does what I want it to do in terms of color and space," she says. "The method produces a result that's so evocative. It gives the entire work a continuity of surface and enables me to work in rich, saturated color."

Ampe's arashi shibori–dyed textiles provide materials for what she likens to collage. "I don't know when I start how they'll end up," she says. "I'll lay ten or twenty pieces on my design wall, and that's the part of the process that's the most fun and feels the most creative." After piecing the selected textiles, she topstitches them by machine and hand. "I like to work in a series of four or five at a time, but it's so time-consuming that rarely happens," she says. Still, she perseveres. "I love working on it and I love feeling it," she says. "Music is the same way. It's very tactile and I love doing things with my hands, things that consume you in time."

Taking pleasure in handwork derives from Ampe's years on her family's diversified farm. "My dad worked like crazy and I helped him in the fields and loved it," she says. "We raised cattle, sheep, ducks who would run to the river and swim away, bees for honey, wheat, rye, a little corn for animals, meadow hay for cattle." The farm was on a hill, surrounded by hardwood forest, with a view of a river valley. The work ethic honed on the farm, along with the views of water, woods, and fields, influences her to this day.

"My work is about nature and landscape, my love of the earth," she says. "Growing up there, I always felt a little excitement, a little anxiety about the weather, about droughts and storms. I get that feeling from being physically in nature and also from music. I'm in the present, and then it's gone."

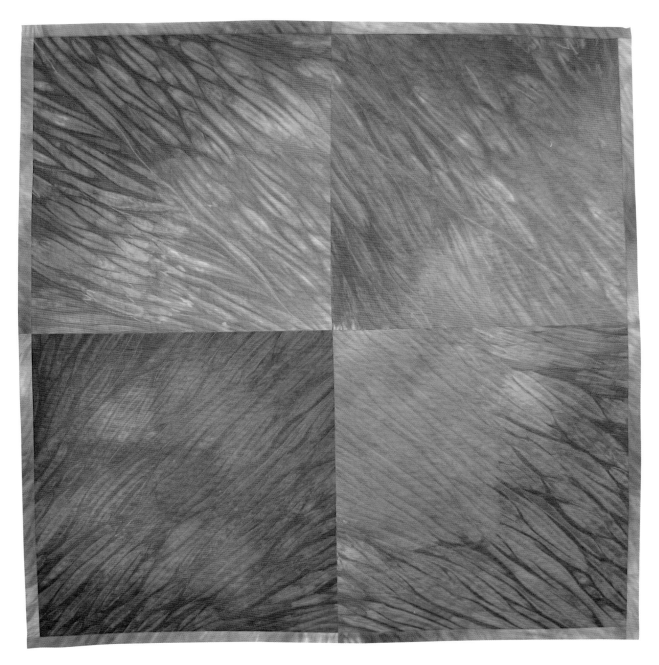

Rye Field, 2011
Cotton, machine-quilted
42 by 44 inches

Colorform 27, 2012
Cotton, machine-quilted
50 by 47 inches

Colorform 27, detail

GAIL BAAR

Buffalo Grove, Illinois

While most midwesterners look forward to winter's end, the change of seasons signals more to Gail Baar than a respite from frigid temperatures. Warmer weather provides an opportunity to replenish her hand-dyed fabric supply, the pieces of which are the starting point for much of her work.

Baar employs the warmth of the sun to intensify colors on the fabrics she colors with Procion dyes. She'll purchase one hundred yards, then individually dye one- and two-yard cuts, hanging them outside to dry. Pieces that appeal to her wind up on her 8-by-8-foot design wall, where the result is rarely what she imagined at the start. These hand-dyed colors fuel her work, as does her focus on shapes. A childhood in Minnesota and travels to South Dakota and her family's cabin on Lake Superior exposed Baar to open sky, barns, massive ore boats, and blue water seemingly without end. "I like shapes that are fairly straight, but not made using a ruler," she says. "I like them to look like someone made them by hand." Baar limits her palette of clear colors within each piece. "Colors help me see the shapes and the relationships between them, but too many colors blur their importance," she says.

Her use of machine quilting is similarly restrained. Most quilts receive matchstick quilting, with lines ⅛ to ¼ inch apart. She values this heavy quilting for the firmness it imparts and compares the resulting textile to a painter's canvas. Her attempts at varying the direction of the stitching have proved unsatisfying. "It looks too busy and interferes with the view of the shape," she says. "I like the simple and straightforward."

Baar started as a traditional quilter, and her transition to art quilting came after viewing an exhibition of the Gee's Bend quilts at the Milwaukee Art Museum in 2003. The quilters' spontaneity in cutting and color placement changed the way Baar worked, as did learning to dye fabric and attending workshops with the Ohio-based quilt artist Nancy Crow. In addition, Baar, a cellist and cello teacher, finds that elements of music—patterns and repeated motifs—influence her compositions. "I've been told my quilts have movement, and I think that comes from being musical," she says. "There are a lot of interesting correlations between music and art."

Colorform 18, 2012
Hand-dyed fabric, batting, cotton thread, machine-quilted
50 by 44 inches

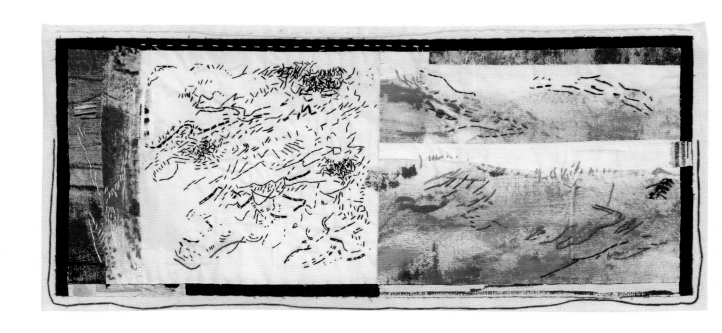

Lake Views 3, 2012
Cotton, acrylic paint, hand-quilted
22 by 10 inches
Photograph by Petronella Ytsma

SALLY BOWKER

Cornucopia, Wisconsin

A move to northern Wisconsin provided the impetus for Sally Bowker's horizontally oriented *Lake Views* series. "I lived by Lake Michigan as a kid, but was only interested in the beach and swimming," she says. "Now we're up by Lake Superior, where seeing the shore, the sky, and the water is so important."

Her work commingles nature's ample elements with its minutiae. "In my earlier work, in photography and painting, I looked all around, then crouched down to get my point of view. I really enjoy representing all aspects of a place."

After a career in library science, Bowker started on the path to art quilts when she earned a BA in art and an MFA in drawing and painting. After twenty years her ardor for painting waned, and around the same time she saw an exhibition of the Gee's Bend quilts. "I was so struck by the life and sense of improvisation in those pieces," she says. "They used these loose, generous shapes, but there was a basic intention behind them."

Bowker tentatively started painting elements of quilts, then learned traditional quilting at a local shop. Workshops with textile artists Ilve Aviks and Dorothy Caldwell provided further inspiration. Bowker's current work starts on muslin, which she paints with acrylics, then appliqués with both commercial and hand-painted fabrics. "I save any scraps larger than a quarter-inch," she says. "Little pieces add a touch of something lively."

Stitching is Bowker's favorite part of the process. "I love the contrast and energy of those little marks," she says. "I work out from an area, building up different weights and densities. Sometimes I take some out. I enjoy this malleable medium that lets me cover up, undo, whatever the piece needs."

The switch to art quilts after a career in painting and drawing wasn't easy— Bowker had to let go of years of effort and her support system, and rebuild her professional resumé. But the timing and the medium seemed right. "I didn't know what this would turn out like, but when you hit a wall you have to go someplace," she says. "I still have ambition, but I'm more relaxed. I feel like I have the space to give this work the time it needs."

Lake Views 5, 2013
Cotton, paper, acrylic paint, hand-quilted
30 by 10 inches
Photograph by John Brandsen, Karlyn's Gallery Print Shop

Winter Water, 2010
Cotton, paper, watercolor, machine-quilted
30 by 40 inches

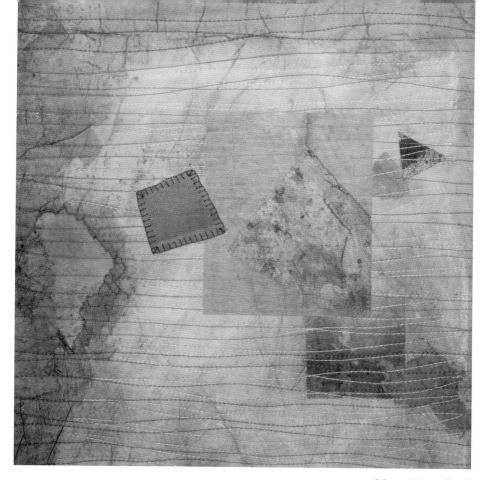

Winter Water, detail

PEGGY BROWN

Nashville, Indiana

Peggy Brown's first foray into watercolor came in the 1970s, when her husband brought home paints. His interest waned, but Brown was hooked. "I became obsessed and worked hard at it, painting every day," she says. People frequently asked if her textural watercolors were on fabric, and the answer was no—until

2002, when a friend taught her to quilt. "I was immediately fascinated," says Brown, who moved from traditional quilting to applying watercolors to fabric.

Brown paints her art quilts on wet silk. "The paint spreads and mingles and mixes," she says. "You never know exactly what will happen and that makes it exciting. That extemporaneousness fits me." She irons pieces to set the paint, sometimes rewetting them to increase the depth of color with additional paint. Once they dry, she adds bits of fabric, or archival tissue coated with acrylic matte medium to prevent tearing.

Brown appreciates fabric as a base because it allows her to work large, as well as for its portability and tactile qualities. Once a top is finished, she layers it with flannel batting and cotton backing, then quilts with straight lines or simple, organic curves.

The Midwest's landscapes and seasonal changes enliven Brown's work, particularly her color choices. *Winter Water* is a memory of ice and snow, created in Florida where she formerly spent half the year. She recently returned to Indiana fulltime. "I love the deep ravines, hills, and ridges where we live," she says.

Brown and her husband, a fine-arts photographer, for years traveled to art fairs to sell their work. Though that's a thing of the past, she still spends time in her studio each day. "It's automatic, it's what I do," she says. "I have so many ideas, I'll never be able to do them all."

When Autumn, 2012
Cotton, silk, watercolor, leaves, digital
images, machine-quilted
42 by 42 inches

Prairie Serenade, 2013
Cotton, machine-quilted
48 by 39 inches

SHELLY BURGE

Lincoln, Nebraska

In *My Ántonia,* Willa Cather's book about life on the Nebraska prairie, there's a line that describes meadowlarks "singing straight at the sun." For Shelly Burge, that phrase resonates. On Burge's family farm, the sound of the meadowlark is a harbinger of spring. "I love that wonderful call," she says. "You recognize it right away."

Prairie Serenade also alludes to the human inhabitants of Willa Cather's Nebraska. "I finished the quilt and bound it, but thought it needed something else," Burge says. She removed the binding and cut six inches off one side of the quilt, adding a panel pieced from homespun fabrics. "I cut off-grain and pieced quickly to represent a utility quilt that a person in a sod house might make from scraps to warm her family," she says.

Meadowlarks aren't the only avian species to appear in Burge's work. Red-winged blackbirds, cardinals, and cranes show up in her quilts. "I love the details in their feathers and their freedom," she says. Dyeing her own fabrics enhances Burge's ability to depict fleeting moments and abstract concepts like sunrise or Nebraska's topography. "The colors, the big sky, the things around me inspire me," she says. The same is true of regional politics, and Burge's quilts address Walmart's growth and the Keystone pipeline expansion. "Quilting is my way of expressing myself, whether it's stories about my family or issues I'm interested in," she says.

Though Burge first learned to sew in childhood, on a hand-cranked sewing machine at her grandmother's home, it wasn't until she married and her husband's grandmother gave them two quilts that she started quilting herself. "I took classes, and the more I learned, the more I wanted to learn," says Burge. She started teaching quilting classes in 1984 and has since taught around the country and internationally.

Quilting in its many forms occupies Burge: she's written two quilting books, volunteers behind the scenes at the International Quilt Study Center in nearby Lincoln, and makes room in her life for all forms of quilting. "I love traditional blocks, but I also love creating my own designs," she says. "I enjoy variety and will go from machine to hand techniques to painting and drawing my own designs to traditional blocks. People ask if I'm a fiber artist. I'm proud to say I'm a quilter, perhaps enhancing tradition by doing contemporary things."

Pumpkin Patch, 2012
Hand-dyed cotton, copper, glass beads,
machine-quilted
18 by 45 inches

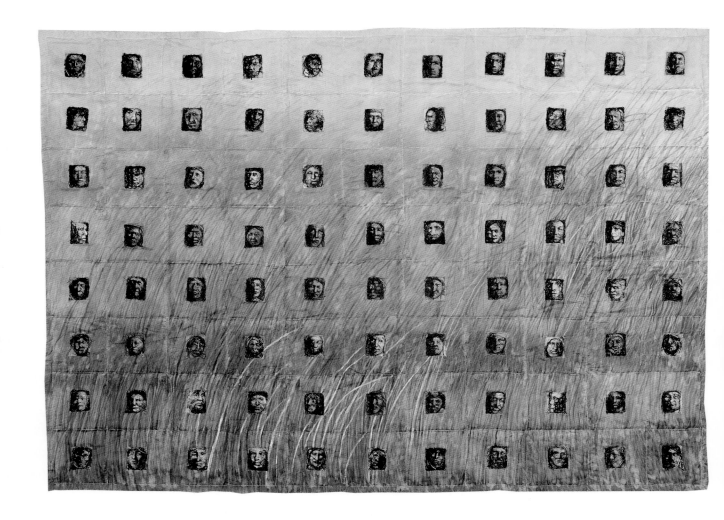

People of the Wind 1, 2009
Silk, wool, metallic paint, rust, oil pastel, digital images,
hand-embroidered, machine-quilted
60 by 49 inches
Photograph by Jim Turner

People of the Wind 1, detail
Photograph by Jim Turner

SHIN-HEE CHIN

McPherson, Kansas

Though she's listed as the sole maker, Shin-hee Chin considers *People of the Wind 1* a collaborative work. The art quilt's base is a worn silk coverlet that Chin divested of feathers, then batiked, painted, and stitched. "I'm fascinated by using old materials," she says. "I'm incorporating the work of an unknown woman. The legacy she left can be recycled and recreated as an art form." In addition to connecting her to other makers, reusing materials frees Chin to express herself without concern about damaging new and expensive goods. "The artist's idea is more important than the medium," she says, a concept she shares with her art students at Tabor College.

Chin embraces unconventional materials and techniques in part because of circumstance. An immigrant to the United States from Seoul, Korea, Chin lived on both coasts before landing in Michigan, then Kansas. "I lost my language, so for a long time I was voiceless," she says. "The visual language of making art became my way of communicating. I was uprooted from my tradition and had the double marginality of being a new immigrant and a woman in American society."

The subject of *People of the Wind 1*—a rough translation of the word "Kansas"— is another marginalized population, Native Americans. Chin chose the piece's overall golden tone to emphasize eighteenth-century Europeans' romanticized notion of Native Americans as "noble savages," as well as because it's the rich color of the prairie on which they lived. To render individual faces, she used gestural, sketchlike hand-stitching, which she prizes over drawing for its ability to penetrate the fabric and create depth. "My needle becomes an extension of my hand, and I enjoy the engagement with my materials," she says, noting that hand-stitching allows her to create more expressive faces and control the pace of her work. In sewing by hand, she also pays homage to women's work. "Sewing machines can be very masculine, making things bigger and faster," she said. "I'm fascinated by taking this feminine activity and turning it into fine art."

Chin finds it's easier to maintain her pace, and explore her art, in the Midwest. "Being in the middle of the United States gives me moderation and helps me stay balanced between Eastern philosophy and Western culture," she says. "I can respect the boundaries of quilt making, but enjoy pushing them to make the work my own."

Lake Autumn, 2012
Cotton, wool, whole cloth, hand-embroidered, hand-quilted
40 by 33 inches
Photograph by Jim Turner

Martello 5: Liaisons, 2012
Cotton, machine-quilted
45 by 32 inches
Photograph by Roger Rowitz

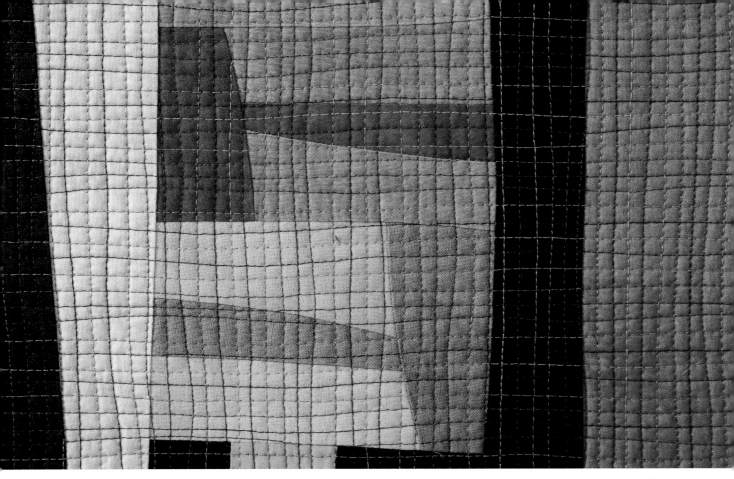

Martello 5: Liaisons, detail
Photograph by Roger Rowitz

SANDRA PALMER CIOLINO

Cincinnati, Ohio

The stereotype of getting a job done in the Midwest involves teamwork: joining forces to raise a barn, bring in the harvest, or stitch a quilt. But Sandra Palmer Ciolino finds she creates best in solitude.

That's not to say she works in isolation. "I like uninterrupted opportunities to make decisions and call my own shots," says Ciolino. "But I also appreciate critical feedback from respected colleagues." That feedback sometimes comes at Nancy Crow's Timber Barn in central Ohio, during workshops that feed Ciolino's interest in contemporary, nonrepresentational work. "When I first went, I felt I'd found my niche," says Ciolino of the classes organized by Crow, the influential art quilter and teacher. "It offered a viewpoint on my art I hadn't encountered in other studies or pursuits."

Ciolino's passage from traditional to art quilter evolved along with an interest in infrastructure. While taking photos, she found herself eschewing landscapes for close-ups. After returning from a vacation without a single shot of family members, she realized her visual interest lay in abstraction. "I'm a detail person, I like minutiae," she says. "This transition from macro to micro was part of my process of finding what I truly love creating."

Ciolino works frequently in a series: she'll explore simple, abstract shapes first, then distort, exaggerate, and elongate motifs in subsequent pieces. This enables her to relax and enjoy the process. "I don't have to solve all the problems in the first quilt," she says. "I know I'll have a chance to try other ideas." (Her pieces are often named for these shapes: *martello* is Italian for hammer, while the translation of *sgabello* is stool.)

A design wall is an integral part of Ciolino's composition process. "It's intuitive and improvisational," she says. "I pick a palette and have a general idea of a motif or overall composition, but it evolves. There's a lot of fabric flying and a lot of editing." Many of the fabrics she uses come from Kentucky-dyer Virginia Keiser and her studio, Color by Hand.

As Ciolino works on each piece, she's also mentally working through ideas for machine-quilting the finished top, which she does on a domestic sewing machine. "I pay just as much attention to that as to the composition," says Ciolino. For *Martello 5: Liaisons* she opted for the subtle nuance of an overall grid in eight different thread colors. In *Sgabello 5: Surveillance,* she chose a variety of patterns, ensuring that particular areas advance or recede. "There are limitless ways to quilt a quilt. My goal is to elevate the quilt's artistry."

Sgabello 5: Surveillance, 2012
Cotton, machine-quilted
69 by 45 inches
Photograph by Roger Rowitz

Building Bridges, 2012
Cotton, machine-quilted by Sheryl Schleicher
65 by 83 inches
Photograph by gregory case photography

KATE GORMAN

Westerville, Ohio

Photos sent to Kate Gorman of family members who'd emigrated from Scotland to Michigan provided the perfect base for her artistic explorations. "For five or six years I've been intrigued with movement, migration, and the not-knowing of the future," she says. She added elements from the landscape of her much-

Bernadette in Artichokes, detail

loved Upper Peninsula of Michigan: birch trees, gulls, and a tempestuous lake. In one original photo, Gorman's great-aunt Bernadette had an enormous bow in her hair. "It lent itself to bird wings and I started from there. I like the idea of magical realism."

Originally, Gorman was an illustrator for text and trade books. She started quilting when her children were young. "I made about three traditional quilts but my corners didn't meet—I'm not someone who likes to draw buildings or cars or straight lines—and I thought 'I'm never going to make it in this world,'" she says. Her home state of Ohio, however, was at the heart of early art quilting and proved the perfect place to explore the medium: Gorman took fiber classes in the early 1990s but continued working in a number of media, including collage and drawing on clayboard.

She's since discovered that combining drawing with fabric gives her effects she couldn't otherwise achieve. "These pieces were drawn with a paint bottle held over the fabric, and I like the way the paint smooshes out in places, adding unpredictability to the lines," she says. "When I started drawing on fabric, I wanted my drawing and hand-stitching to relate to one another. On *Uncle Bud*, I wanted the stitches to be reminiscent of the other marks I made and vice versa. On *Bernadette*, the coarseness of the fabric and the unfinished edges are essential to the piece—it wouldn't have looked the same on paper or clayboard."

While Gorman's past influences her subject matter, her present has contributed to changes in technique. She is one of three studio artists helping clients with developmental disabilities create artwork that generates income at Columbus's Goodwill Art Studio and Gallery. "There are several Goodwill artists who do line drawings all the time," she says. "The looseness of their approach was very inspiring. Taking risks and experimenting has opened up for me since I've worked at Goodwill. My work still looks pretty organized and controlled, but I'm not going at it with the same mentality. I'm freer now."

*The Closing of the Calumet
and Hecia Mine, or Uncle Bud
Heads South,* 2013
Linen, acrylic paint,
hand-quilted
21 by 45 inches

Hoagy Carmichael Sampler (Stardust), 2009
Hand-painted with acrylic on muslin, hand-quilted
35 by 32 inches
Photograph by Tom Van Eynde

Hoagy Carmichael Sampler (Stardust), detail
Photograph by Tom Van Eynde

DONNA JUNE KATZ

Chicago, Illinois

Donna June Katz's work methods don't leave much room for spontaneity. But rather than fighting her media—paint thinned to a nearly translucent, dye-like consistency on unbleached muslin—she values the planning it necessitates. "It helps me focus and refine my ideas in advance," she says.

Those ideas draw on carefully researched depictions of the natural world. Though Katz lives and works in downtown Chicago, flora and fauna inspire her. "Celestial bodies, geology, and rivers are the kind of things that make me sit up and take notice," she says. "I find forms that are affected by the laws of physics especially interesting." Time spent as a docent at Chicago's Field Museum increased her knowledge of paleontology and brought her into regular contact with fossils. She's recently embraced birding and notes that even in Chicago, along Lake Michigan, there are birding areas where the surrounding trees and vegetation seem almost bucolic. "I spend a lot of time there, picking up leaves and seedpods to sketch," she says. "Nature awes me more than most things."

Maps also intrigue Katz and show up in her work. "They appeal to me because they're simultaneously representational and abstract," she says. "I like the fact that they exist on various levels."

For an exhibition of quilts inspired by music, Katz created *Hoagy Carmichael Sampler (Stardust),* incorporating Carmichael's lyrical references to his home state of Indiana, the Wabash River, and various birds. Also depicted are leaves of Indiana's state tree, the tulip tree, and postcard views of a Wabash river town and a riverside landscape. The border's inner contours derive from Wabash River maps. Rather than using stitches to emphasize portions of the piece, Katz applied them randomly to create texture.

Though Katz has sewn since childhood, it wasn't until she'd finished her undergraduate and graduate studies in painting and printmaking that she returned to working with cloth. "I thought it would be difficult to sell paintings and drawings so I tried hand-painted pillows, which I sold through museum and gift shops," she says. She added wall hangings, and these morphed into the quilts that became her artwork. She is drawn to art quilts for their tangible quality. "They have a presence that flat images lack," she says. "They're an object as well as an image."

End Moraines/Lifeforms, 2007
Hand-painted with acrylic on muslin, hand-quilted
33 by 33 inches
Photograph by Tom Van Eynde

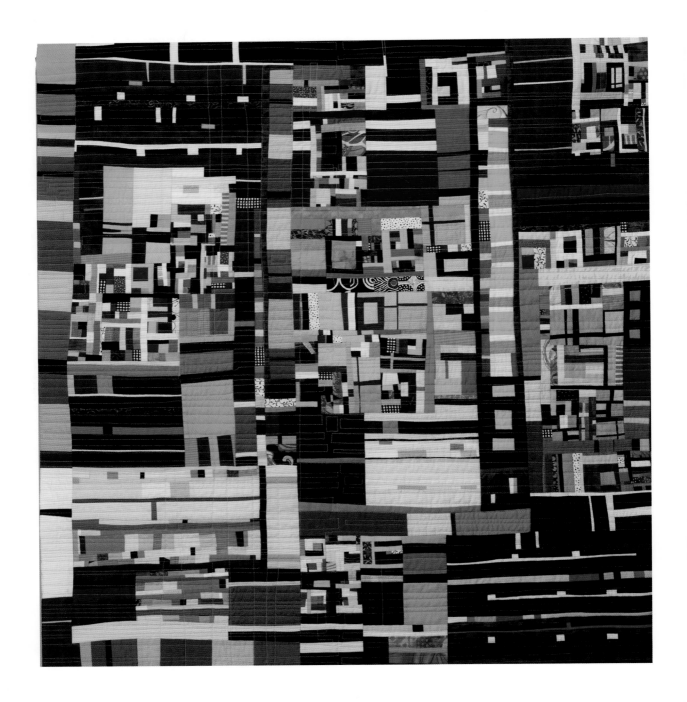

In Vino Veritas, 2012
Cotton, machine-quilted
40 by 42 inches
Photograph by David Roberts Photography

BETH MARKEL

Rochester Hills, Michigan

Beth Markel shared her childhood bedroom with her grandmother, who was born in 1884. "She'd been quilting a long time at that point," says Markel. "Every morning I'd thread needles for her. She was the most meticulous quilter I've ever known, sixteen stitches to the inch. To sit under her feet when she was quilting was to be in a magical place."

In Vino Veritas, detail
Photograph by David Roberts Photography

Despite this familiarity with textiles, Markel was first drawn to ceramics. "I grew up with my hands in my art," she says. Then her father gave her a camera. "It taught me to open my eyes and really look around, at the large scale and the small and everything in between."

Photographs she took while picking concord grapes in Marine City, Michigan, were the inspiration for *In Vino Veritas*. "There were so many purples and greens and I appreciated the depth of the colors, the sun moving across the vines, the way the shadows changed on and under the leaves," says Markel. "Walking along holding the sharp scissors, I paid attention to detail. To recreate that, I sewed and cut and sewed and cut until there were intricate, busy places, along with the wide-open areas. That's what it felt like standing there."

In Vino Veritas and *Escúchame* were created with a freeform technique that Markel's explored in recent years. "I've set aside rulers and it's just me and a rotary cutter and a sewing machine and a wall of fabric," she says. "It's been freeing to work without a preconceived notion of the end product." Inspired by her family's "making do with what you have" dictum, these pieces also use fabric remaining from other projects. These changes in Markel's techniques coincide with a heightened sensitivity to music, to her garden, and to events large and small around her.

Though Markel's quilting might surprise her grandmother and the others in her family who quilted before her—Markel is a fifth-generation quilter—she finds it the perfect means of expression. "When I was making ceramics, I loved that tactile quality," she says. "Working with fabric is the happy marriage of the visual of photography and the tactile of ceramics. My move into art quilting has been about finding my own voice and having something meaningful to say."

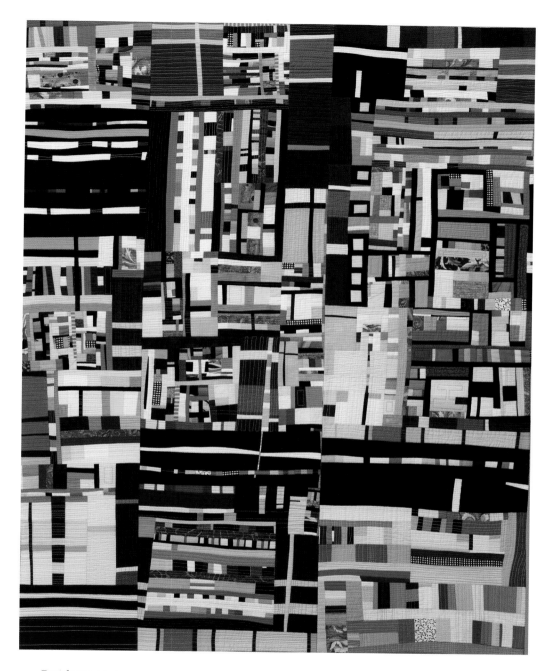

Escúchame, 2012
Cotton, machine-quilted
39 by 51 inches
Photograph by David Roberts Photography

Twisted, 2011
Cotton, aluminum rod, eyelets,
rubber grommets, machine-quilted
60 by 14 inches
Photograph by Rion Núñez

Twisted, detail
Photograph by Rion Núñez

DIANE NÚÑEZ

Southfield, Michigan

At exhibitions of Diane Núñez's three-dimensional artwork, she's often asked the inevitable "Is that really a quilt?" question. She'll explain that just like a traditional quilt, her work has three layers sewn together. "It is a quilt, but you have to think differently, and I think differently," says Núñez.

An art quilt can also include nontraditional fibers, and the metals and mesh that Núñez incorporates into her work connect to her days as a jeweler. "I did a lot of knitting and crocheting with wire," she says. "I used fiber techniques with metals, and now I'm using jewelry techniques in quilting."

Twisted grew from Núñez's observations of the topography and geography of her home state of Michigan, particularly its rural rolling hills and the resulting changes in light and shadow. Her palette of hand-dyed fabrics includes influences of the bright greens of the city and suburbs where she grew up and the blues from her parents' lake home. "Every time I try to do something monochromatically, I never finish it," she says.

Though her work includes industrial elements, Núñez achieves her colors by hand-dyeing 100 percent cotton fabrics. "Texture is important," she says. "It has to feel right to use."

Núñez, a landscape architect who appreciates mathematical precision, takes pleasure in working in three dimensions, but finds shipping and exhibiting these works to be challenging. She builds models of her pieces to work out armature and attachments before creating the final piece, and many of her quilts come apart for shipping.

One such piece, *Diagonal 3 x 3*, has been hung in different shows both diagonally and on the square, and was once hung from the ceiling. "I tell people to hang it in whatever way appeals to them, and I enjoy going to a show to see how it ends up," she says. Núñez created another piece from three-inch squares that snapped together and could be changed at the viewer's whim. "A woman bought it to wear as a stole, and I would never have thought of that," she says.

This flexibility seems appropriate for an artist for whom instructions are little more than a place from which to diverge. "I'm not someone who follows recipes very well," says Núñez. "A pattern for me is simply a base to work from."

Spaces, 2011
Cotton, synthetic microfiber, stainless steel slat,
stainless steel cable, machine-quilted
33 by 51 inches
Photograph by Rion Núñez

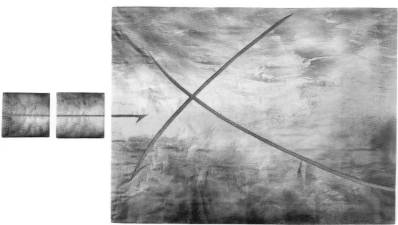

Landthreads: Sightlines, 2010
Polyester, machine-quilted
120 by 38 inches
Photograph by SAQA and gregory case photography

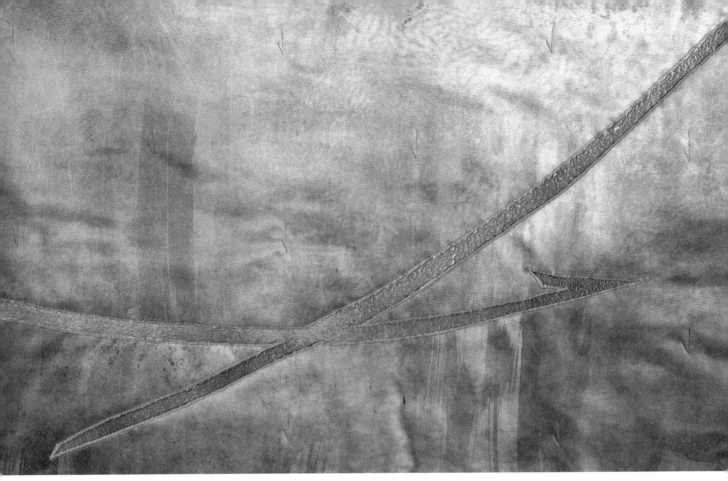

Landthreads: Sightlines, detail
Photograph by SAQA and gregory case photography

PAT OWOC

St. Louis, Missouri

Pat Owoc expresses herself through imagery both concrete and ethereal. While outwardly dissimilar, both affirm a reverence for the West Kansas land where she grew up and for those who inhabited the land before her.

Though Owoc learned to sew as a child and pieced a few traditional quilts, a workshop in disperse dyeing was the gateway for the work she continues to do today. Her first pieces in this medium depicted the view toward Colorado from her childhood home, a horizon that continues to provide inspiration. "It's a landscape like no other," she says. "You can stand in many places and turn 360 degrees and see almost forever. There are trees, windmills, and occasional homesteads, but you can see so far you lose detail, which gives it a dreamlike quality." It also fuels her imagination about those who came before her on the land, including settlers, Native Americans, and buffalo.

Owoc's representational *Stories* series considers pioneers who endured privation, hardship, and loneliness. "It's a rich story, particularly of the women who had so much to contend with," she says, acknowledging the adversity her own forebears endured.

Her *Landthreads* series honors the physical territory on which they lived. This work shares an affinity with the landscapes of J. M. W. Turner, the English painter of light, though Turner depicts a geographic world far from Kansas. Owoc had begun her color explorations when she saw his paintings and felt a kinship. While Turner achieved his luminosity with paint, Owoc accomplishes hers with dye on polyester fabric. She prepares papers with disperse dyes, then selects from as many as 150, blending hues to create the fabric that forms the basis of her *Landthreads* work. She creates the "blades" that intersect the pieces by cutting away sections of the front to reveal a second layer fused beneath. "The distinct, sweeping lines create gates that open to stories, ghosts, time, history, and memories," she says.

Though Owoc's lived apart from her beloved western Kansas farm for many years—she resides in St. Louis, where she worked as a high school teacher and counselor—she feels deeply connected to the land owned by her parents and their parents before them. "When I go back, there's one particular hill," she says. "I come up over that rise and look at the land, and I'm home."

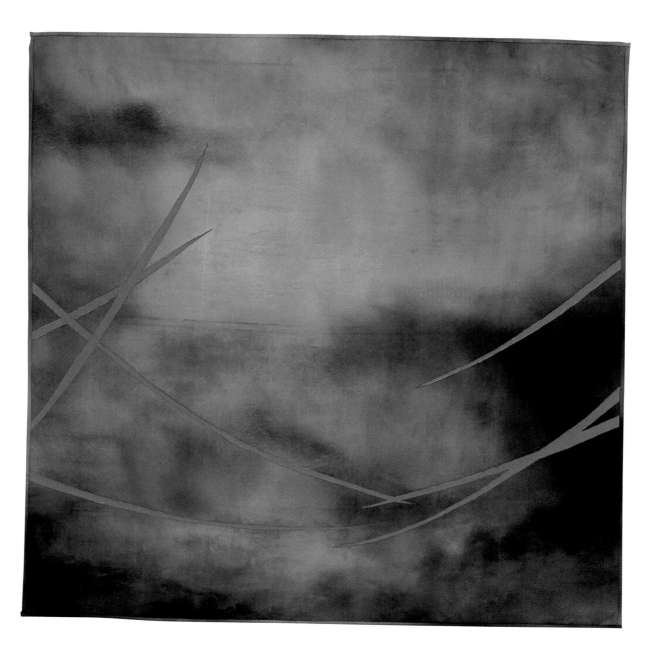

Return, 2009
Polyester, machine-quilted
51 by 52 inches
Photograph by Casey Rae/Red Elf, Inc.

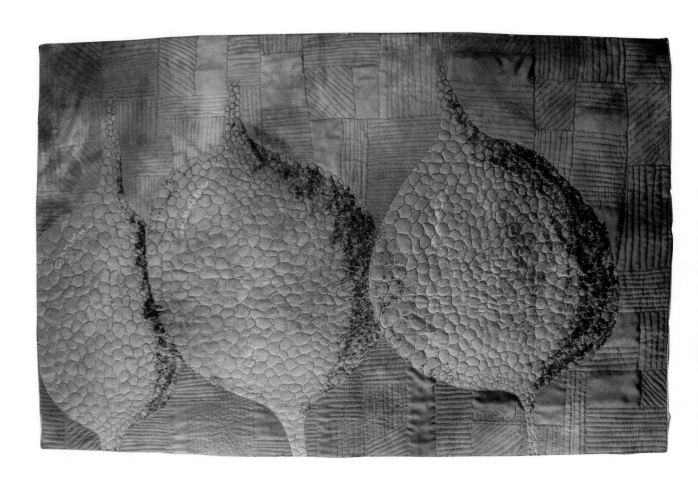

Goldenrod Galls 2, 2011
Silk, machine-quilted
28 by 20 inches

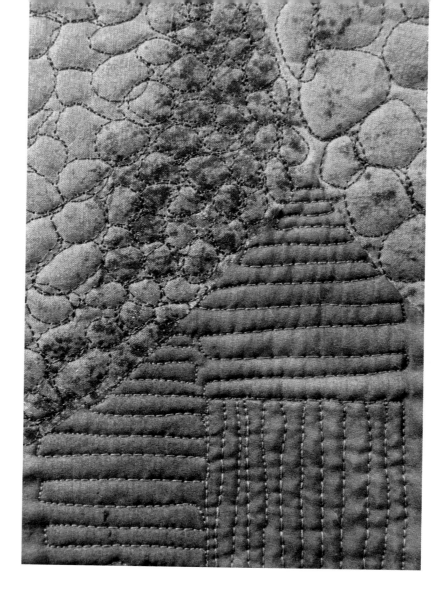

BJ PARADY

Batavia, Illinois

Walking fifty acres of restored prairie as a Nature Conservancy volunteer in Keokuk, Iowa, provided inspiration for BJ Parady's *Goldenrod Galls* series. "In the winter, especially if the prairie had been burned the previous year, it would be all dark colors so you'd notice the texture of things," she says. "Galls—swell-

Goldenrod Galls 2, detail

ings on a stem of dried goldenrod—were persistent and stood out against the absence of everything else."

This attention to natural detail melds Parady's degree in botany with her studies in art. While working as a laboratory technician after college, she took watercolor classes and learned the basics of design and composition. Around the same time, she learned to make traditional quilts. What she calls "an innate problem with following a pattern" meant that her conventional quilts were soon disrupted with curved lines and uneven grids. A tornado that ripped through Hamilton, Illinois, where she lived in 1999, was the fulcrum for a shift in her creative aspirations. "Twenty-three houses were destroyed in my neighborhood and I wanted to express that in art, and fiber was my medium," she says of the pieced and appliquéd triptych that resulted.

Learning to hand-color fabric added to Parady's repertoire, and she enjoys the spontaneity and "happy accidents" inherent in dyeing and painting. When an idea strikes, she sorts through her previously dyed yardage. "The fabric speaks to me and I take it from there," she says. "It's kind of intuitive. I don't think deeply about it, although a lot of pieces hang on my design wall for months before I figure out how to resolve them." Free-motion quilting provides variation and contrast: the pebbling pattern on the *Goldenrod Galls* series was inspired by stones at the edge of Lake Cooper, adjacent to the Mississippi River's Lock and Dam No. 19. She layers paint and hand-stitching atop her quilting.

Parady's work evokes the power of the midwestern landscape through abstract and atmospheric elements of the seasons, landforms, plant remnants, and the prairie. "We don't have mountains, but our landscape is more relatable on a personal level," she says. "On a prairie, you can become engulfed in grasses taller than you are, and at the same time you have vistas and a low horizon. The Midwest gets a bum rap as flyover country. Part of what I'm trying to say in my quilts is that we have an unappreciated ecosystem that needs to be celebrated."

Goldenrod Galls, 2011
Silk, machine-quilted with hand-stitching
20 by 36 inches

Of Bogs and Benthos, 2011
Silk, velvet, brocade, embroidered
52 by 72 inches
Photograph by Tom Van Eynde

Text visible within the artwork:

"a Bog, quagmire or mire is a type of wetland that accumulates acidic peat, a deposit of dead plant material."

"1880-carp introduced 1665-Eurasian watermilfoil invades Madison lakes"

Lake [Mendota]

"drought"

"An invasive species is a species that is non-native to the ecosystem and whose introduction causes or is likely to cause economic or environmental harm. Invasive species can be plants, animals or other organisms. Human action are the primary means of introduction"

"Eutrophication a body of water acquires a high concentration of especially phosphates and nitrates"

"a Macrophyte is an aquatic plant In lakes they serve as a nursery area for larval fish and a habitat for macroinvertebrates"

"Lake Monona"

"2000"
"2002"

Of Bogs and Benthos, detail
Photograph by Tom Van Eynde

BONNIE PETERSON

Houghton, Michigan

Bonnie Peterson explores issues ranging from breast cancer to war crimes, from climate change to domestic violence. "I'm a rabble-rouser at heart," she says. "I don't work on anything unless I care about it."

Of Bogs and Benthos juxtaposes hard science—graphs, measurements, and definitions—with luxurious fabrics and threads. The piece resulted from a collaboration between artists and University of Wisconsin Center for Limnology scientists to increase awareness of water research and information through the arts.

While Peterson incorporates images to tell her stories, text also plays a prominent role. Dropping the feed dogs on her sewing machine, she forms letters by guiding the fabric under the needle. Included in *Of Bogs and Benthos* are concepts she learned during the collaboration. "I don't expect people to take notes, but I thought if someone read just one definition and later heard it on a news report, they might pay attention," she says. In her other pieces, text includes journal entries from long-ago explorers and environmentalists like Ernest Shackleton and John Muir, reflecting Peterson's love of history and the out-of-doors.

Her work also dips into history with its nod to the traditional crazy quilt. The freedom of those quilts, their intricacy and blending of textures, appeals to Peterson, and she employs a variety of stitches and threads to secure irregularly shaped pieces of velvet, satin, silk, and brocade. Sections of quilts—graphs, imagery, and words—may stay on her design wall for weeks as she decides how best to incorporate them into a piece.

Peterson, who has an MBA and formerly worked in market research, lives in the Upper Peninsula of Michigan, where she can step outside her door and cross-country ski much of the year. But she spent most of her life in Chicago, and it was there that she earned a grant from the Illinois Arts Council. "It came at a time when I wasn't sure if I wanted to keep doing art, and it gave me a huge boost about feeling that my work was worthwhile," she says. She remembers standing at an exhibition that featured her early piece about breast cancer and hearing people titter about bras on the quilt. "Then they'd get closer and see it was about cancer and I'd linger and hear them talk," she says. "It's so satisfying to bring issues out into the open."

Within the embroidered artwork:

Phenology is the study of the timing of natural events. Phenological records provide comparisons between and among geographic regions include the date of emergence of leaves and flowers, the first appearance of birds. Examples of migratory phenomena are very sensitive to small variations in climate, phenological records can be a useful proxy for temperature in historical

Lake Mendota
duration of annual ice cover

days of ice cover: 160, 120, 80, 40, 0
Year: 1850, 1900, 1950, 2000

Bonnie Peterson

Ice Phenology, 2011
Silk, velvet, embroidered
12 by 28 inches
Photograph by Tom Van Eynde

Knowledge, 2012
Photograph digitally printed on cotton, hand-quilted
15 by 15 inches

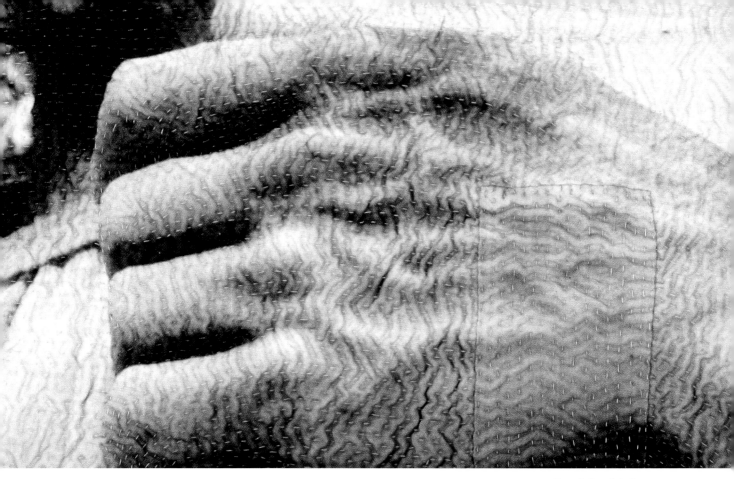

Knowledge, detail

LUANNE RIMEL

St. Louis, Missouri

The passing of time is central to Luanne Rimel's work, and St. Louis's Bellefontaine Cemetery provides a focus for her temporal explorations. "I am drawn to the sculptures that stand as guardians of midwestern history," she says.

This fascination with cemeteries and those who came before extends beyond

St. Louis. For a recent birthday, in lieu of a party, she asked for a new camera lens and a trip to "a really good cemetery."

"Cemeteries are an interesting reference to whatever town we're in—you learn how old a community is and who was important," she says.

Rimel's influences combine her passion for history and travel with modern technology. The advent of inkjet printers enabled a fabric less stiff than those she'd created by hand-painting on silk in the 1980s and by printing on fabric in a darkroom in the 1990s. A visit to Japan in 2005 introduced her to *boro*—the patched and mended clothing and household textiles stitched from the 1700s through the early twentieth century—and her fabric of choice shifted from silk to flour-sack towels, which link to domestic practices and personal memories.

"Growing up, we six kids did the dishes every night, and though I hated doing them we'd sing, talk, and listen to the radio," she says. "When I met my husband's family they were very quiet, but after dinner we'd pull the drawer open and there would be bleached and embroidered flour-sack towels. I'd dry and his mother would tell me stories. The dishtowel became a conversational conduit." Rimel's piecing is a nod both to women who mended and repaired textiles and to necessity; it's the way she's able to create larger works from the fabric she produces on her seventeen-inch-wide inkjet printer.

While Rimel's imagery is planned, her stitching is not. In an effort to catch and reflect light, she hand-stitches patched pieces both horizontally and vertically and changes thread colors. The stitches create shadows and textures that allude to the marking of time, and each piece changes shape as threads are drawn through the cloth. "When I start, I don't always know what the stitching will do until I stop and put it on the wall," says Rimel. "As it firms up, it pulls the picture into hyper-focus. The entire process is interesting to me."

The Glance, 2013
Photograph digitally printed on cotton, hand-quilted
15 by 15 inches

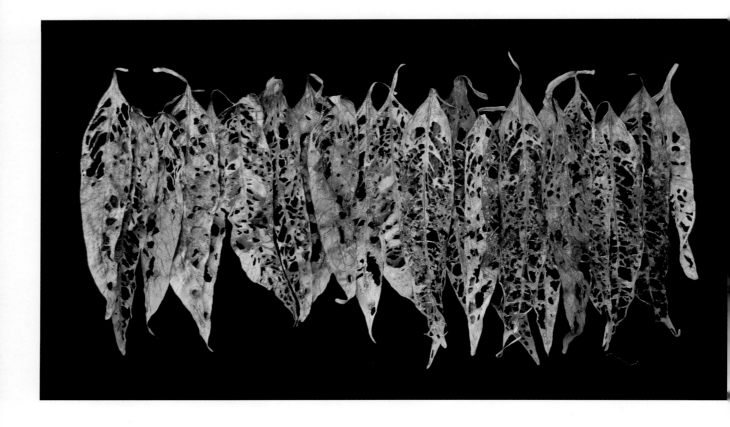

Leaf Fall, Variation 3, Fragments, 2010
Cotton, digitally manipulated and printed, stiffening liquid,
free-motion machine-quilted
55 by 32 inches

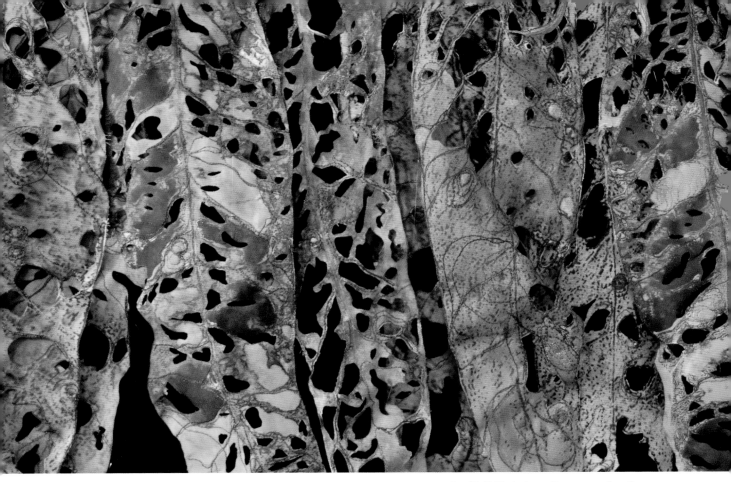

Leaf Fall, Variation 3, Fragments, detail

BARBARA SCHNEIDER

Woodstock, Illinois

Barbara Schneider's work reflects her midwestern surroundings through the Japanese aesthetic of *wabi sabi*. This appreciation for the moment, imperfect as it may be, shines through in *Leaf Fall, Variation 3, Fragments*, a glimpse of the detritus of autumn. "I make these things both because I'm intrigued by them and so people can see how beautiful they truly are," she says.

Schneider's work often starts with long walks through conservation areas near her Illinois home. "Being outside soothes my soul, and when I'm walking, in particular, is when I get my best ideas," she says. For her *Leaf Variations* series, she collects flat and curled leaves, often during their autumnal coloration, and scans them. She's fond of the skeletal remains of linden leaves, eviscerated by Japanese beetles. "I enlarge them so that people can see the details and that they're much more than just a dead leaf," she says.

Schneider uses Photoshop Elements to magnify and occasionally enhance the leaf's coloration. With a thirteen-inch-wide printer, she reproduces these images on fabric, sometimes printing half at a time and marrying the halves by fusing. She adds batting and varying amounts of backing and stitching to create emphasis. For a piece like *Leaf Fall, Variation 3, Fragments,* she goes back and cuts holes to reflect the leaf's fissures. A stiffening glue painted on the front and back helps the leaf hold its shape, and Schneider may add additional stitching. If she's not happy with the outcome, the leaves can be dampened and reshaped.

A related method involves collaging fabrics to create the front of the fabric leaf, then stitching and using a needle felter to poke holes and soften, recreating leaves' decomposition. "I try and get the effect any way I can," says Schneider.

Schneider has worked in graphic design, the book arts, and papermaking. Her move to quilts came in 1996. "I learned traditional techniques, but it wasn't long before I did what I wanted to do," she says. "The leaf pieces feel as though my work is coming back around—they're somewhere between paper and fabric."

For *Mingled Water* and her *Reflections* series, Schneider photographs the moments when light hits water on the rivers, ponds, and streams she sees near her home or while traveling. "Those reflections aren't even there, they're just something your eye sees and the camera sees better," she says. "To me, these ephemeral moments really matter."

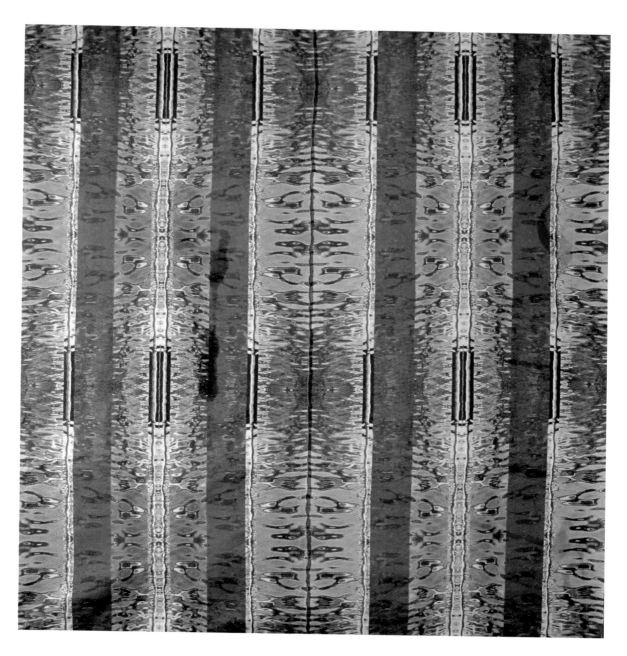

Mingled Water, 2013
Cotton, digitally printed, free-motion machine-quilted
72 by 72 inches

Rain Garden: Ace of Pyrex Cups in the Kitchen Tarot, 2011
Whole-cloth cotton, fabric paint, airbrush, airpen,
mostly machine-quilted
91 by 60 inches

Rain Garden: Ace of Pyrex Cups in the Kitchen Tarot, **detail**

SUSAN SHIE

Wooster, Ohio

Storytelling of the personal and political kind is at the heart of Susan Shie's work. Her subjects, ranging from world figures like Nelson Mandela and Barack Obama to friends, family members, and pets, often appear in the same piece. "They're together because that's how we think: the big issues, the middle-sized issues, the personal issues," she says.

71

Rain Garden: Ace of Pyrex Cups in the Kitchen Tarot exemplifies this combination. Work at her alma mater, Wooster College, led to the development of an organic product that purifies chemically polluted water. "If we don't fight to save the earth, nothing else matters," says Susan. "This miraculous thing was created in my hometown." Typical of her work, *Rain Garden* includes snippets of text about the product, current events, and Shie's life. "Some people may read some or all of it, others none," she says. "But even unread, it has to contribute to the composition."

Shie's current work grew from her undergrad days, when she painted on unstretched canvas because it was easy to transport and store. In graduate school, she created "soft paintings," cutting and piecing canvas with stitches and knitting. "I thought of that as cave-girl sewing," says Shie. She embellished pieces with embroidery and beading, but eventually chose to emphasize imagery over stitched elements. "I wanted my stitches to be art marks, electric and full of energy, but they were becoming tinier and I was becoming more of a sewer and less of a painter."

A turning point came when she learned to push fabric paint through an airbrush. "As long as the airbrush and paint are working well I feel like a hummingbird, dancing and floating as I swoop slowly along," she says. Though she spends weeks developing a topic and making preliminary sketches, the moment comes when she faces her fabric to create her imagery freehand. "It's scary at first because that sets the scale, but once that's over it's all good." She later adds writing, manipulating its size and texture to create movement. Stitching is the final part of the process.

Though Shie identifies as an outsider artist and painter, it's important to her that she creates with fabric. Working on unstretched canvas as an undergrad was a practical matter, but a lecture by the feminist and artist Miriam Shapiro helped Shie to consider the connections between her art and women's work. "I want to show softness, empathy, nurturing," she says. "A quilted painting is a user-friendly object."

The View at Our Kitchen Window: 7 of Potholders in the Kitchen Tarot, 2012
Whole-cloth cotton, fabric paint, airbrush, airpen, markers, mostly machine-quilted
35 by 35 inches

House 11, 2012
Cotton, digital images, tied
22 by 47 inches

House 11, detail

MARTHA WARSHAW

Cincinnati, Ohio

When Martha Warshaw set up her studio in 1997, she was torn between textiles and the three dimensions of ceramics. In the end, textiles won. "With fabric, there are infinite possibilities with pattern, materials, and scale," she says. "It's more ephemeral than fired clay and comes with the cultural trappings of 'women's work,' which can be a plus or a minus. But it seemed like a place to start."

Dimensionality, however, continued to intrigue her. Warshaw's *House* series has its roots in small cardboard boxes she dismantled to better understand their construction. Each of these pieces folds into the same house form, but Warshaw chose to display them in two dimensions, each laid out differently. "They create energetic patterns in the way they unfold, tumbling along," she says. "They're also fun little puzzles to work out in my head."

The fabric Warshaw employs is derived from the old textiles she collects. She photographs the pieces, tweaks the images in Photoshop, and prints the results via Spoonflower. "I do this because I love these things, I love the wear and tear," she says. "Sometimes a quilt is dreary and worn out, but I can separate an 8-by-8-inch patch from the sad whole of it and make an interesting, abstract pattern." Warshaw's quilting is largely invisible—she'll hide tiny stitches in the seams or sew over an area in the fabric that already depicts stitching. "My work is all about piecing and the ideas of quilting," she says.

Warshaw's other influences include her parents; her mother tried needlework in all its forms, and her father took up photography in middle age. "I absorbed his pleasure in the work he did and the way he took the craft of photography and turned it into art," she says. Museums, from the artwork itself to the way it's displayed, are also inspirational. Fragments of mosaics and shreds of fabric, beautifully mounted, speak to her. "Things that aren't whole anymore are still very evocative," she says.

Warshaw collects similar bits and pieces. Her fabric stash consists of yard goods and garments she's found at thrift stores and yard sales. She notes that while few today are required to sew, these fabrics and her own work connect her to a time when they were. "Doing this artwork is very different, but nevertheless a way of continuing that necessary work," she says. "I'm aware of being a part of that legacy."

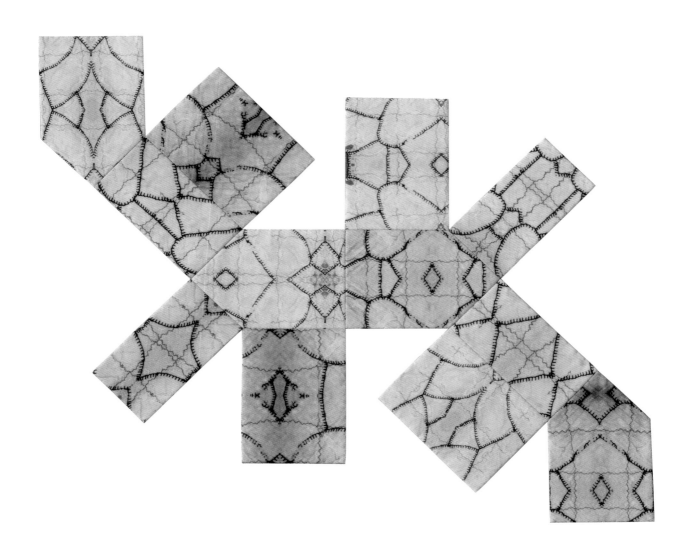

House 10, 2012
Cotton, digital images, tied
25 by 29 inches

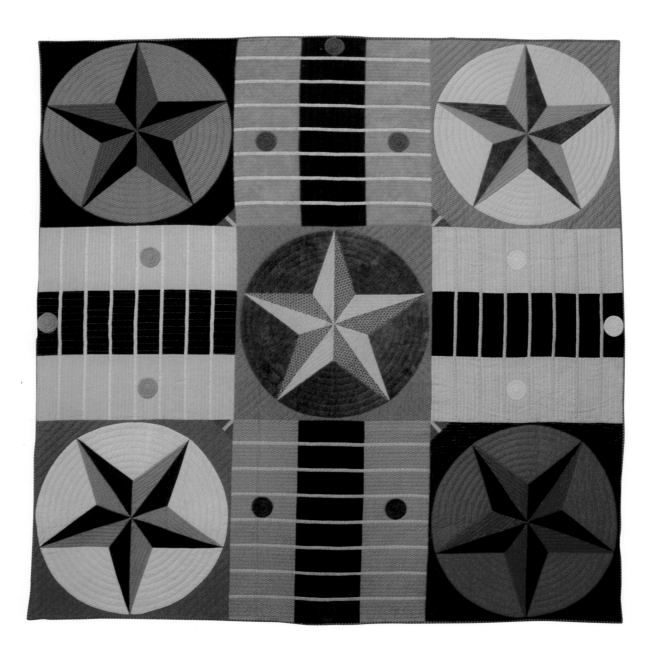

Venus Transit, 2012
Cotton, hand-quilted
96 by 96 inches

Venus Transit, detail

ERICK WOLFMEYER

Iowa City, Iowa

Despite its Pop Art sensibility, Erick Wolfmeyer's *Venus Transit* was inspired by a magazine article on old-fashioned game boards. "I didn't know Parcheesi," he says. "I thought the image was exotic, like some Sufi divination board." He named the piece *Five Stars* for the shapes he appliquéd to the pieced top, but on the night he finished it the planet Venus appeared to move across the sun—and Wolfmeyer renamed the quilt for that rare celestial occurrence.

Though he was born in Missouri and is now a resident of Iowa, Wolfmeyer connects to places beyond the prairies. He's drawn to the West, and the seven years spent living in South Dakota's Black Hills are the closest he's come to feeling truly at home. "My sense of place is very tentative," he says.

That comes in part from Wolfmeyer's past. Given up for adoption at seven months, he's spent much of his life coming to terms with loss. "Women lose kids, kids lose moms," he says. "I'm working it out through my quilts."

Wolfmeyer—who has a BFA in photography—was first smitten by quilting when he stitched a baby quilt for a friend in 1998. "A quilt is portable and very forgiving and I love the feel of fabric," he says.

Though the inspiration for Wolfmeyer's quilts doesn't always come from the Midwest—many are dreams of places he misses or imagines—he finds Iowa the perfect locale for making them. For years he lived in a small town and drove a school bus to support his art. He has since moved to Iowa City and holds a full-time job, but still lives frugally. His intensively pieced quilts can take up to six months to complete—*Portmanteau,* its color palette inspired by Iowa's winter landscape, has 2,888 pieces—and he creates them one at a time in his 565-square-foot home. Midwestern Amish quilters hand-quilt his finished tops. Wolfmeyer's quilts have been included in numerous shows: he was one of five quilters invited to travel to China in 2012 as part of the U.S. Embassy–sponsored exhibition *The Sum of Many Parts: 25 Quiltmakers in 21st-Century America.*

Though midwesternness doesn't drive Wolfmeyer's work, he's happy that *Venus Transit* found a home with friends in St. Louis's Soulard neighborhood. "The metal stars on old brick buildings are their neighborhood symbol," he says. "The stars on the quilt connected to *their* sense of place."

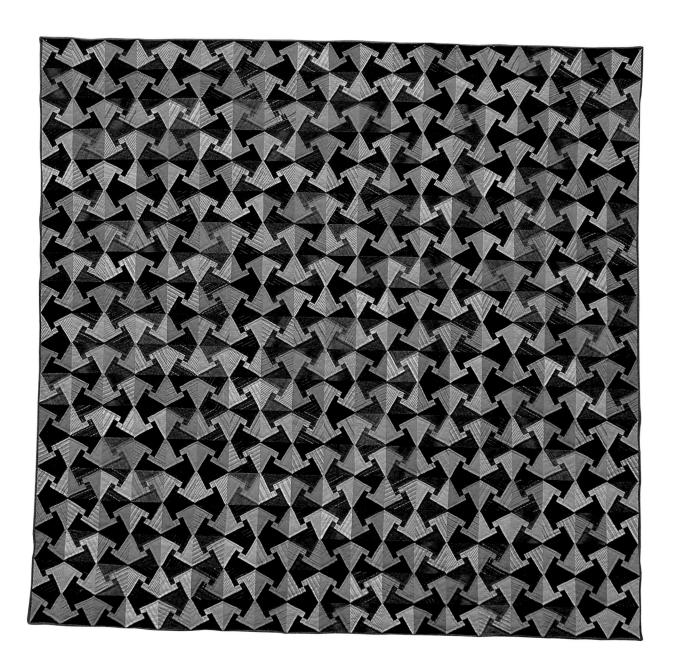

Portmanteau, 2011
Cotton, wool, hand-quilted
93 by 93 inches

OTHER BUR OAK BOOKS OF INTEREST

Always Put in a Recipe and Other Tips for Living from Iowa's Best-Known Homemaker
By Evelyn Birkby

A Bountiful Harvest: The Midwestern Farm Photographs of Pete Wettach, 1925–1965
By Leslie A. Loveless

Down to the River: Portraits of Iowa Musicians
By Sandra Louise Dyas

Neighboring on the Air: Cooking with the KMA Radio Homemakers
By Evelyn Birkby

Nothing to Do but Stay: My Pioneer Mother
By Carrie Young

Patchwork: Iowa Quilts and Quilters
By Jacqueline Andre Schmeal

A Peculiar People: Iowa's Old Order Amish, An Expanded Edition
By Elmer Schwieder and Dorothy Schwieder